Speak French Now

Student, Trave

CH00448762

It is not by rules of grammar that one learns to speak French, rather it is by improvising French as a 3-4 year old does, by speaking French words and phrases and adding to and changing them as one goes. It is a more natural way of learning.

If you can't speak French you don't know French!

©2022 Ralph Carroll Hedges

Contents

Foreword

Education has been built on the premise that information per se, with its tests and measurements, is the guide to the success of a program of study, where but one answer is the correct answer even while words and phrases change with context, therefore there cannot be but one 'correct' answer. Even dictionaries provide several contrasting definitions of the same given word according to the use of the word.

In contrast, books I, II, III, and IV of Speak French Now, are predicated on the educational philosophy that improvising French words and phrases as the *only way to learn French*. A practical definition of improvisation is *choices* - nothing more nothing less. Life itself for example, is an improvisation made up of choices, all unscripted.

Yet, ask any professionals, not part of the 'system' and they will tell us that the way to learn to write, for example, is to write ! – or, the way to speak a foreign language is to speak ! Why is this such a difficult concept to understand by those who create the language charts of verb tenses, and parts of speech, with phrases that illustrate a particular word which must be memorized and graded with little or no effort in actually speaking the language contextually ?

Speak French Now Book I, provides a foundation upon which you may speak French on the most basic level, able to improvise on French words and phrases, including French numbers, asking or giving the time of day, French math for shopping in euros, greetings, and personal and historical dates, including birthdays, known as 'anniversarie'.

Learning to Speak French

This book is oriented to speaking French by accumulating words and phrases that may be improvised and enlarged upon. In the beginning, there will be few choices due to the lack of a vocabulary, and this is where a dictionary becomes essential. There are three dictionaries that you must acquire. Each dictionary has its own uses, where if you don't find what you are looking for, one of the others may have it. The Webster's New World French dictionary is excellent. The Merriam-Webster French-English dictionary is also excellent, and also highlights French Canadian terms. The 'Larrouse unabridged French dictionary you must have as it is the most comprehensive. You will be referred to all three during your studies. Two other books you might find fascinating are, The Great Nadar and Eating and Drinking in Paris. Nadar was a famous 19th century photographer in Paris. Included in the book are photos of well-known people of the time including Gustave Flaubert, George Sand, Nadar himself, Baudelaire, Delacroix the artist, et.al. Eating & Drinking in Paris is a guide for French food and drink. It explains the food and drink terms as found in restaurants with their translations. It's quite thorough and provides a great trip though the culinary arts.

And one more important item... to be successful in any endeavor you must have a set schedule for study. For your French sessions you must schedule a time that is regular, and once set, stick to it without fail, whether it's a half-hour, three hours or more, and when that time comes start your French study. Don't let anything interrupt that schedule. A casual effort won't work, where maybe you'll study and maybe not.

Allons-y! (Let's go!)

Your first job is French pronunciation. Rarely is it anything like its spelling, however make an effort to memorize the spelling of all French words. Diacritics are essential for both the correct spelling of French words and also their correct pronunciation. The 'accute' accent is used only for the letter 'é', with a forward slash above the letter, and changes it's pronunciation from 'eh' to 'ay', as in 'docteur en médicine'– [doctuer emaydsin], where the first 'é' is pronounced 'ay'. [maydsin] A back slash on 'è' is a 'grave' accent and is pronounced 'eh', as in très bien, - very good, [trebieh]. Note also that the emphasis in on the final few letters of the phrase. French words have many silent letters, 'h' is mostly silent, as it sometimes is in English, where the English word 'hour' is pronounced 'our' with 'h' being silent. 'hour' in French is 'heure', and likewise is pronounced with 'h' silent; 'Œr', ou (or) [ewr]. 'homme' – man ou mankind, also is pronounced [om], 'h' being silent. August- août [u], yes, 'u', as in 'douzéjem août' –12th of August [duzjem-u]. ('j' pronounced as 'y') These examples are given so that you may understand what you will be working with. Pronunciation of French words should be close as possible, along with the correct spelling of all words including diacritics. For the acute accent – highlight the 'e', press option, then 'e', and 'e' again. For the Grave accent, highlight the e, then option, then '~' top left of your keyboard, together, then e again. Or, 'insert', then 'advanced symbols' and they will be there as you scroll down. Also, search 'French diacritics' for further help if you wish. 'Copy and paste' is also an option; highlight the phrase or word then 'option' with 'c', then place the cursor where it is to be placed and hit 'option' 'v'. It's a time saver.

Day and night greetings

'Bonjour' [bozur] 'bon' (good) + 'jour' (day), is the most often used greeting by the French. The letter 'j' is like 'z'' as in 'measure'. 'n' is not pronounced. The greeting is used during any part of the day, mornings through the evening. Speak this greeting aloud, adding various French names to whom the greeting is directed makes it personal. Search 'French names'. Merely memorizing it serves no purpose. Many names are pronounced differently in French than in English, for example, 'Charles' is [sharl], likewise 'Herbert' is [ayber]. 'h' is not pronounced in most French words. Go about your business saying the greeting to yourself throughout the day. Get the phrase in your tongue, your head, and speak French aloud. French names become part of your French vocabulary. Parle plus française! [parleplufransay] - Speak more French! Comme Toujours! [comtuzhur] – As always. When pronouncing French phrases, insert the phrase within the [   ] then speak it quickly and meaningfully. 'Bon jour' is not the way. [bozur] is. Then, either [bozurMarie] ou, [bozurePheeleep], or any name you choose – all as one unit as you would in English.

'Bonne nuit' [bonuee]. 't' and 'e' at the end of French words are generally not pronounced. Look up 'nuit' in your dictionary and you will find it's a 'nf', meaning it's a feminine noun. In French that's important, since now 'bon' must be spelled, 'bonne', the extra 'e' is the feminine adjective modifying the feminine noun, nuit, and again, bonne pronounced [bo], the same as in 'bon', but understand that 'silent' letters may seem to be pronounce because of what comes after. In the case of 'bonuit', the 'n' may seem to be pronounced. Add names to this greeting and say it aloud expressively, as though you meant it. This greeting will be useful at night when turning in. Always add names – Bon nuit, père! [per], - dad, ou, mère, [mer] – mom, ou grand-mère [granmer] grand-mother, ou, mémé, etc. Look up and research words you don't know, as you would for unfamiliar English words.

'Bon soir' [boswar], 'good evening'. In your dictionary 'soir' is 'nm', a masc. noun, therefore 'bon'. [bo] Look up 'soir' in your dictionary. The pronunciation will be in letters in the [bracket]. There will also be sentences in the dictionary that use the word. Make a note of the easier ones, the ones that you feel you could pronounce and use and improvise upon. Limiting your work to the words and phrases in this book is but a fraction of your work in learning French. Look up all words that are unfamiliar. Build your vocabulary that way. Make a list of your vocabulary in alphabetical order so that you may track your progress. You will remain a 'beginner' until you have reached a substantial vocabulary of several hundred words. With that vocabulary you can say you know French, 'un peu' - a little [ewpew]. It takes time and a huge amount of dedicated effort.

Soir nm [swar] Evening. 'Journal du soir' – evening paper. [zurnaldu**war**]. Bon soir, monsieur! [boswar, mes**ewr**] – Good evening, sir! Bon soir,…add several names, improvise! In your browser, put in this or any phrase with a name and have it translated to French, then listen to the French sound-byte and create your understanding of its pronunciation in [   ]. Say the phrase repetitively but with different names.

Soirée nf [swaray] It is a feminine noun, therefore 'bonne' [bo]. An evening event. [bos**waray**] is also 'good evening', but could refer to an event; a celebration, party, etc. 'Une soirée de concert' [unswaraydko**cer**] - Evening concert. soirée dansant [swaray da**sa**] – evening dance. 'Bonne soirée' The next to last 'e' has the necessary diacritic, é, pronounced, 'ay'. The final 'e' isn't pronounced – it's a feminine ending.

Revoir *vt* (verb transitive; takes an object) [revwar] is a verb, 'see again', 'au' is 'to', and 'au revoir' is 'to see again', like the English 'review', 'look again'. 'au revoire' [ow revwar] is, 'see you again, or simply, 'bye', ou 'see you' often used in the phrase, 'au revoire, et bonne soirée' [ohrevwarebos**waray**] – 'Good bye, and have a good evening'. Saying these phrase, as you probably are doing now, is not nearly enough. They must be practiced and improvised upon until they are French expressions said by a French speaking person – you! Please remember that French phrases are not etched in stone! They may easily be altered, changed, only part of the phrase said, like your party has departed and all you can say is just, 'soir'! Think how you communicate in English and that will give you a clue communicating in French.

This serves as an example of improvisation by combining phrases. Now, you can really start talking French when you might say, 'au revoire Jean, et bonne soirée'. [ohrevwar zha eboswaray]'. You have the choice of words to use in the phrase, and when you use the different words you are improvising the language with choices, therefore it will stick, unlike merely memorizing one version of the phrase. Talk aloud the phrase and add different names. Write the phrase including diacritics, (é) several times. Then talk it throughout the day. Do the same with all phrases in this section. It's all about repetition with the improvisation of phrases. Parle française! [parle fransay]. Speak French! If you look up 'parle' you won't find it, because it is the 'present' form of the basic infinitive, 'parler', to speak. You can ask your browser, 'conjugate parle', and it will give you the whole grammar of the word, which you really don't need right now. It will, however give you the basic, infinitive, 'parler' from which the present, future, and past may be constructed...later.

'Salut!' [salu] The ending 't' is silent. 'Hi!', even 'bye!' Salut, Charles ! Comment vas-tu?' [saluCharl, comavastu] - Hi

Charles ! how are you?, ou 'how have you been? Ou 'Salut Marie ! quoi de neuf ?' [saluMarie, kwadenewf]– Hi Marie, what's new ? 'neuf' may be the number 'nine', but as an adjective (adj) it means 'new, fresh, even young. Look the word up in your dictionary. Parle le en française ! [parlayahfransay!] – say it in French. 'Salut' may be used to say goodbye to friends – 'Salut Peter e bonne journée' - 'bye Peter, have a nice day' [SaluPeter, ebozurnay] Note that 'journée' is not the same as the English, 'journey'; they are, 'faux ami', [foami] false friends. 'Day' in French is 'jour' ou 'journée'. 'Bonjour' is used when first greeting someone, and 'bonne journée' when they're leaving. [bonzhurnay] Get used to the difference by trying it in different situations. Refer to the English part of your dictionary to separate one definition from another. Avoid being confused by such seemingly equivalent words that are not even pronounced the same.

'Salut' may be used both when seeing a friend , and when leaving. 'à bientôt!' Is another great farewell greeting. [ahbietoh] Look it up! When would you use it? Also, when would you use 'bonjour', and bonne journée? When you understand usages you understand French.

Résonse: [rayspa] 'ça va' [sava] 'It's Ok' ou 'pretty good', noncommittal, ou 'pas mauvais, merci!' [pamovay, merci] - Not bad, thank you! Look the words up in your dictionary. Ou, 'je vais bien, merci'[zevayzbie,mersi] – I'm well, thank you. Look up each new word and include them in your *memorized* alphabetical vocabulary. Improvise by using different words for different situations. For example, when could you use 'mauvais' vs 'bien', ou pas bien ? Think about these differences and apply them in French sentences of your choosing, testing your sentence in a translator, then listen and practice, - its French. *C'est très important* ! – look 'em up... [sestreimporta] – all together, not separate words.

Bonne après-midi, madame [bonapraymidi, ma**dam**], singular. [me**dam**], plural. Good afternoon medam/ladies. Look up all unfamiliar words, including those used in the definitions, àpres, for example, listed as: 1. Prép (French for preposition), same as English, preposition, just pronounced differently. [prayposizjo] -'j' pronounced like 'y' as in **ye**llow. Followed by (a) gén (général) same as English but pronounced [zaynayral] – 'g' like 'z'. aprés coup - after the event. [apraycu] This is the general definition. And, 2. adv – its usage as an adverb; 'deux jours aprés' – [dewzursapre] Two days later. These distinctions are vital for you to understand as you look up words. Your dictionary is the source of your new words and your understanding, and pronunciation.

Ciao! [tshao] – Bye! The word is borrowed from the Italian. Not really used much today as it was 10-15 years ago.

à plus [ahplu] - later! …when you're in a hurry. 'Pas plus' [paplu] – no more, ou 'non plus' [noplu] – no more. ou 'non plus, merci beaucoup' ! [noplumercibocu] – no more, thank you very much. There are different ways of translating French to English since they are quite different languages. When saying a phrase, think of it as a French phrase rather than a translated phrase. Another great phrase is, à bientôt [abjetoh] - See you soon! (the 'j' here is pronounced 'y' as in 'yellow') See you soon, Jean! [abietohzah] Snipetsofparis.com is a really fun site that's all about Paris. Check it out!

Adieu [adjew] …for when you want to be dramatic. Such as, 'Adieu bon amis' [adjew boami] – goodby dear friend! 'adieu' lit. is 'with god' and not used in normal conversations. Look up 'bon, bonne' for its many uses. Keep them in mind because you may need them. 'amis' is a 'nm', masc noun therefore use 'bon'. [bo] …some include the 'n' and the 's'… [bonsami] as it seems to 'roll' better.

Another greeting that works well is, à demain [ahdemay]– see you tomorrow, ou, à demain soir, ou matin, ou, nuit. – see you tomorrow evening, morning, or night. And to add further improvisations, you might add, 'a domain, et bonne soirée' – see you tomorrow, and have a good evening ! – or the reverse, 'bonne soirée, à demain, ou, 'bon soir', bon nuit à domain [bonuiadomay] – good night see you tomorrow. etc. This is improvising the language, not just memorizing words and phrases. Work these choices, copy and paste in a translator, and listen carefully to the pronunciation of your phrase. And, btw, listen to the English pronunciation, then the French pronunciation of the same phrase. The English will sound perfectly normal, while the French may be barely understood. I have news for you... to a French speaking person the French will sound perfectly normal while the English will hardly be understood !

You now have several phrases and words in your vocabulary. It's just a beginning, but all trips start that way. Write all phrases with various names with correct French spelling. Then, *parle le en française!* – speak it in French, ou *dis-le en française* [disleahfransay] – say it in French. 'dis' comes from the basic infinitive, 'dire' to say – look it up. French is capitalized in English but not in French, (français) nor 'English' (anglais) [aglay].

Research all words, spelling, pronunciation, *nf, nm, v*t, V (voir), etc.. Give yourself an education. And then review, review, and review, and don't stop until all greetings become easy to pronounce and improvised upon. Change (improvise) phrases with different names, people, countries, etc.

These phrases should be available for you at any part of the day or night. If not, revoir! [revwar] (look it up, and compare *au revoir*) Also, speak phrases quickly with meaning, as a French person would, not hesitatingly word by word. Listen to French speakers in reverso, Google or most any translator.

Section II: Getting acquainted

Question [kestjo]: 'Hello, what is your name?' – Bonjour, comment t'appellas? [bozur, comatapela]. 't' is a contraction of 'tu', you. 'comment' here, is not the same as 'comment' in English, therefore, a 'faux ami'. Look up 'comment' in the English part of your dictionary for the word in French. If you don't carry through on questions such as this you could be confused, leading to incorrect usage, or no usage at all. Also, make a note of French phrases used as examples in your dictionary that you might want to use. There are several for 'comment'. Expand your French as your go and research all words, and listen to all sound-bytes for pronunciation. Also, less formally, 'quel est ton nom?' [kelestona] - What is your name? Use these two phrases alternatively and with various names. You can always add, 's'il vous plais' [sivuplay] – if you please, or simply 'please'. So, 'Bonjour, monsieur /madam /madmoiselle /junge homme/ bonhomme - comment vous s'appellas, s'il vous plais ? Or, comment vous s'appelas, monsieur, ou, quel est ton nom, s'il vous plais ? 'tu' is used for family and close friends, 'vous' is used for those to be respectful of. Languages have options, choices… use them and learn from them, they are *your* French. In a 5x7 notebook or smaller, add the phrases you are using so that you have them when you want to practice them. Add your pronunciation in a bracket [   ].

Résponse: 'Je m'appelle John' [zhemapelezah] …and with your own name. …or less formally, 'mon nom est John' monomeszah]

Question : Who are you, and what is your name? Qui êtes-vous, et quel est vôtre nom ? [kietevoo, ekelesvotrnom] Say these expressions quickly, as a unit not just one word at a time. Say them as a French person would, as a real question. – [kietevu, ekelesvotrnom]

Résponse : 'je m'appelle Pierre]'. 'I am called Pierre' ou, 'I'm Pierre' 'Je suis Pierre' [zshemapel Pier] ou, '[zshesui Pier] 'm'appelle' is a 'reflexive' term, lit. 'I call myself'. In your browser look up reflexive verbs…use your own name, and various names to get used to saying the phrase. You won't find 'suis' in your dictionary, so ask your browser to 'conjugate 'suis'. You will find much there that you don't need yet. However, you will find what infinitive verb it comes from, and that will be valuable information.

Question : 'Où êtes-vous né ?' [ooetevoo nay? – Where were you born? 'né' is 'born'. Look it up. It is also used when indicating a married woman's born name; 'Mrs Williams née Smyth…' The extra 'e' is a feminine ending due to a woman's name. Look it up, ou ask your browser. Get involved with your French. Mere memorizing gets you nowhere, and will be doubtful that you will remember, or be able to use that which you have 'memorized'. Always be curious! – être curieux toujour! [etrecuriutu**zur**] (listen to a sound-bite in a translator)

Résponse: 'Je suis né à Paris' [zhesuee nay a paree] I was born in Paris. Add several French cities to get used to the phrase. Do some research of French cities. And, you might add to it, 'mais je suis espanol'. – but I'm Spanish. Putting them together with various names, cities, and nationalities; 'Je suis né à Paris, mais je suis espanol' This combines two phrases with various names, improvised, so you learn and understand the phrases. So, 'Je suis né à …' add a city or country, then add, 'mais je suis…' add a nationality. And your own situation? – Where were you born and what nationality are you? It might come in handy. Get really familiar with the phrases. In the 'dates' section following soon, you will give your birthdate along with where you were born …it's one thing at a time.

… parle plus Française! [parlayplu fransay!] Research! – rechercher [reshersche] comme toujours! [cohmtuzhur] – As always !

Question: Where are you from, and what is your name ? This combines two phrases that you already know. 'où êtes-vous né, et comment vous s'appellas ?' [ooetevunay, e comavusapele], ou – [ooetevunay e comatusepele] You can always add s'il vous plaît if you chose. 's'appelle' is another reflexive verb, lit. 'how do you call yourself'. Be sure to look up reflexive verbs. This is improvising - choosing what to say, or not to say. 'vous' is the term to use that is respectful. 's'il te plaît' is for close friends or relatives. 'vous' and 'te' are both 'you'. What you say and to whom you say makes a difference, especially in France. So.. 's'il vous plait, monseiur' vs. 's'il te plait, mémère'. [sil teh plai] 's'il' is a contraction from 'se + il' if + it 'plait'-pleases. It's a wonderfully polite phrase. If you look it up you won't find it since it is a conjugated form of 'plaire'. Look it up. Now you have three phrases to use when wanted. Use them! Say these words expressively so they make sense.

Résponse: Je viens du paris, et m'appelle es Jean' – I'm from Paris, and my name is Jean. [zhevenduparee, emapelezha' The root word for *viens* is *venir*, 'to come'. 'viens' is the present tense. 'je viens', [zeveh] is 'I'm coming'. Take care to spell all French words correctly, and with diacritics.

Say word spelling aloud, 'app elle', appelle [apel], etc, since the spelling of words rarely match their pronunciation.

Question: Do you speak French? – parlez-vous française ? [parlayvoofransay]

Résponse: Oui, je parle française, mais juste un peu. [owee, zsheparlayfransay, may zshustupew] Yes, I speak French, but just a little. ou – Oui, je parle juste un peu française. [owee, zheparlezhustapoewfransay] Here you have two new words, 'mais' and 'juste'. Spell them, pronounce them, research them! They may contain a phrase or two that you will be able to use. Speak the two versions above interchangeably. Get well acquainted with all French phrases by speaking them aloud repetitively *and improvised.*

One more word in regard pronunciation... the emphasis occurs on the last part, ou vowel of a word viz., s'appelle – [s'ap**pel**], personne – [per**son**], ou on the last part of the last word in a sentence, s'il vous plais – [silvu**play**]

Please note that phrases are pronounced as a unit, not separate words, and the whole unit is that which you need to say without difficulty, otherwise it's not French !

Add other languages to the phrase. You'll probably have to ask your browser, 'What is (the language) in French? – and you will have them. Also, listen to their pronunciation and add them to your alphabetical vocabulary.

Section III: Ladies and Gentlemen

Bonjour mesdames et messieurs! [bozewermedam emesewr]
Hello ladies and gentlemen!

Bonsoir monsieur! [boswar mesewr] Good evening, sir!

Bonjour madame! [bozewr madam] Hello, madame, ou, Ms.

Bonjour mademoiselle! [bozewr madmwazel] Hello, miss!

Excuse me sir, what is your name please? - Excuze-moi
monsieur, quell est vôtre nom, s'il vou plait? ou, ~ comment
vous s'appelez, s'il vous plait? [excoosemwamesewr,
kelesvotrnom, seevuplay? ou ~ comment vous t'appelles
~[excoosmwamesewr, comavutapella seevuplay]. What words
you use depend upon to whom you are speaking. Look up 'tu'
in your French dictionary. Be aware of what circumstances you
would use 'tu' vs 'vous'. Yes, it's important. Don't embarrass
yourself!

Réponse : No problem sir, I'm André. Pas de probléme
monsieur, je m'appelle André. (reflexive)
[pahdeprobleymmesewr, zhemapeleandray]. And, use the
alternate phrase for 'my name is...' Review it above if you've
forgotten it. Research 'pas', especially pas[2]. The French
negative will be taken up later, as it is different than English.

Question: Pardon mademoiselle, est-ce votre sac ? [pardah madmwazel, es-se votrsac] - Pardon, miss, is this your bag? ou - parapluie [parapluee] – umbrella, etc. Look up and find various items that you my use in this phrase, then add it to your vocabulary. Also, use other names; monsieur, madam, etc. There are several possibilities for this phrase for improvisation. Be sure to add new words to your alphabetical vocabulary. You should shoot for 100 words, then 200…500… and above. Until you get 500+ words, vous étes débutant ! [vuaytedaybuta] 'étes' comes from the root word, 'être'. Look it up, and look for it in the blue section of the Larousse French dictionary. It's the second item; vous étes. [vuayte]. Also, look at 'je suis' and 'tu es'. When would you use 'tu es' vs 'vous étes'. And, check out the pronunciations.

Résponse: Qui, merci, c'est mon sac. [uweemerci, sesmosac. Yes thank you, it is my bag. ce est – 'it is', *must* be elided to c'est. In English, either way; it is, or it's.

Search other items and add them to your vocabulary, then talk the phrase a dozen times during the day. Look up, *e rescherche* and all new words. Phrases may be short or made into sentences, but it's all about combining words and phrases that you already know. Phrases may have new words for you to research. and that builds '*un vocabulaire*'. [uvocabular] – a vocabulary, votre vocabulair – your vocabulary.

uis improviser! [pisimprovisi] – then improvise ! Look up puis' – there may be phrases in your dictionary that you might use. Write them and speak them. Souvent et fréquemment ! suvaefraykemo] Look 'em up! Note the difference between peu souvent' and 'plus souvent'. [pusuvah] vs [plusuva] Be curious ! - être curieux !

Question:, Waiter, please – monsieur/madam/madmoiselle s'il vous plait... un menu s'il vous plait. Avoid using the word 'garçon', boy, as it could be demeaning, even racist. Be sure, if you do use it to add the s'il vous plait. However, when in Paris never use it under any circumstance ! Monsieur ou madam ou mademoiselle est le plus sûr. – is the most sure, i.e. safest. Spell all words aloud, then pronounce them.

Utiliser et souvent. [utilizeesuva] Look up new words and their pronunciation, and use them wherever you can. *Pas si difficile* !

Section IV: Numbers

This is the largest section in this book since they are used so frequently; for shopping,

in finance, anniversaries, and time of day. They can and must be mastered – fully!

There are two basic types of numbers: Cardinal; one, two, three, etc, and Ordinal; first, second, third, etc..

The Cardinal numbers:

Ordinal Numbers:

1. un, une [Œ] ou [ew] , [un] [premje, jer] (j=y)

$1^{er}/1^{er}$ premier/première

2. deux [dew]

$2^e/2^{nd/(e)}$deuxième/second(e). [dewsjem/segah]

The 'e' is for all ordinal numbers

as the abbreviated 'ème' ending

3. trois [trwa   ]

3e troisième [trwasjem] ('j' as in

yellow)

4. quatre [katr]

4e quatrième [katrjem] Note that the 'è' Is with a grave accent, 'eh'

5. cinq [sahk]

5e cinquième [sahnkjem]

6. six [sis]

6e sixième [sizjem]

7. sept [set]

7e septième [setjem]

8. hui(t) [ui] (i=ee)   8ᵉ huitième [uitjem]

9. neuf [newf]   9ᵉ neuvième [newvjem]

10. dix [dis]   10ᵉ dixième [disjem]

11. onze [onz]   11ᵉ onzième [onzjem]

12. douze [duz]   12ᵉ douzième [douzjem]

douzaine, nf [douzay] dozen. Demi douzain – half dozen [demidousay]

13. treize [trayz]   13ᵉ treizième [trayzjem]

Compare 'trois', 'three' et 'treize', thirteen – [trwa e trayz] 'dix et trois égal treize', 'aussi dix et six égal seize', - they are quite similar. – et 'dix et cinq égal quinze'. Spell and say them aloud. From 17 there will be two numbers; dix-sept - seventeen. (dix, 10 + sept, 7=17) *pas difficile* !

14. quatorze [katorz]   14ᵉ quatorzième [katorzjem]

15. quinze [keyz]   15ᵉ [keyzjem]

16. seize [siyz]   16ᵉ seizième [seizjem]

17. dix-sept [dis-set]   17ᵉ dix-septième [dis-setjem]

18. dix-huit [dis-uwi]   18ᵉ dix-huitième [dis-uwitjem]

19. dix-neuf [dis-newf]   19ᵉ dix-neuvième [dis-newvjem]

20. vingt [vah]   20ᵉ vingtième [vahtjem]

21. vingt et un [vahteyewn]   21ᵉ vingt et unième [vah etunjem]

22. vingt-deux [vah-dew]   22ᵉ vingt-deuxième [vah-dewsjem]

...etc. through 29. Write and speak them all...

30. trente [tret]   30ᵉ trentième [tretjem]

31. trente et un [tret eh un]   31ᵉ trente et unième [tretehunjem]

...etc. through 39. Write and pronounce them all aloud

40. quarante [karaht]   40ᵉ quarantième [karahtjem]

41. quarante et un [karatejun] 41ᵉ quarante et unième [karatetunjem]

...etc through 49. ...finish...

50. cinquante [sahkat]   50ᵉ cinquantième [sahkwatjem]

51. cinquante et un [saykot ejun] 51ᵉ cinquanteetunième [sahkot eyunjem]

...etc. through 59. ...finish...

60. soixante [swasot]   60ᵉ soixante et un [swasotetun]

61. soixante et un [swasot ejun]   61ᵉ soixante et

unième[swasotehunjem]

62. soixante-deux [swasot-dew]   62e soixante-deuxième

[swasotdewsjem]

...etc. through 69. ...finish...

70. soixante-dix [swasot-dis] 60+10   70e soixante-dixième

[swsot-disjem]

71. soixante et onze [swasot e ahz] 60+11   71ᵉ soixante et

onzième[swasotetonzjem]

...etc. through 79 ...say and write them.

80-99 French uses a special system for these numbers called the 'vigesimal' system whereby the base is 20 instead of 10.

Therefore, 'quatre-vingt' is 4(20) i.e. 4 x 20, not 4 + 20.

Quatre-vingts is 4x20=80, but vingts-quatre is 20+4=24.

...yeah, I know !

80. quatre-vingt [katre vah] 4(20)=80   80ᵉ quatre-vingtième

[katr-vahtjem] 80th

81. quatre-vingt-un [katr-vah un] 4(20)+1   81ᵉ quatre-vingt-

unième [katr-vah-unjem]

...finish through 89. Work on each of them and learn them well!

90. quatre-vingt-dix [katr-vah-diz] 4(20)+10   90ᵉ quatre-vingt-

dixième [katrvah-dizyem]

91.quatre-vingt-onze[katr-vah-ahz]4(20)+11   91ᵉ quatre-vingt-

onziem [katrvah-onzjem]

...etc. through 99.

100. cent [sah]   100ᵉ centième [sahtjem]

101. cent un [sahewn]   101ᶜ centunième [sahtunjem]

... finish all to 179, be sure to get all pronunciations correct.

180. cent quatre-vingts – 100+4(20) = 80 [sakatrvah]

180ᶜ [skatravahtjem]

181. cent quatre-vingts-un 100+80+1 = 181 [saqatrvaunjem]

Use the vigesimal numbers 180-199 the same as 80-99 and just
add 'cent'. [sa] ... yes, do them all, written and correctly
pronounced. It's French, hey!

200. deux cents [dew sa]   200ᵉ deux centième [dewsatjem]

...finish as before to 299. Yes, all 999 ...the only way to learn
is to do them !

300. trois cents [twasa]   300ᵉ trois centième [trwasatjem]

400. quatre cents [katrsa]   400ᶜ quatre centième [katrsatjem]

500. cinq cents [sanksa]   500ᵉ sinq centième [sahnksatjem]

571. sinq cents soixante et onze 500+60+11 571ᵉ sinq centième

soixante et onze

1000. mille [mil] Write and talk the entire amounts, 1000-2000.
How else are these numbers supposed to be learned ? Yes, this
takes effort, and a lot of it to learn French. The next section will
use these numbers. If it's easy, you have done your work, but if
it's still difficult... do them again, and again ! – until easy.
Révision si necessaire.

Section V: Dates: Historical

1700. mille sept cents [mil set sah] – 1000+7+100 =1700...etc., ou dix sept cents 10+7=17 +100. [disetsa] – [dis-set-sa]

1789. dix-sept quatre-vingt neuf [dizset-katrvah newf] – dis-sept=17, quatre-vingt 4x20=80 + neuf (9) = 89.

14 July 1789 - Quatorze juilliet dix-sept quatre-vingt neuf – ou, mille huit cent quatre-vingt-neuf. [kaytorz zhulieh], etc.

The Bastille, a state prison and symbol of the *Ancien Regime* tyranny, fell to the people of Paris on 14 July 1789, marking the beginning of the revolution. The square where the Bastille once stood is now is now the home of one of the Paris' opera houses, known as l'opéra-Bastille. Ibid p 117

La nuit du 4 aout 1789, the night during which feudal privileges were abolished by the "Assemblèe consituante" (considered to be one of the starting points of the French revolution. Ibid - La nuit du 4 août 1789 – The night of 4 August 1789

1792. mille sept cent quatre-vingt-douze [mil-set-sah-katr-vah-duz] ou…

dix-sept quatre-vingt-douze – seventeen eighty (quatre-vingt) + twelve = 92

La journée du 10 août 1792 - day on which a popular uprising led to the fall of the king and the creation of the *Commune Insurection-nelle* in the place of the *"Commune de Paris"*, marking the beginning of the *Terror*. (Larousse French Dictionary page 67) - La journée du 10 août 1792 – The day of 10 August 1792. [lazurnay dudis u dis-set-kuatre-vah-duze]

1800. dix-huit cent [dizuisah]

1800. mille huit cents – (one) thousand eight hundred – ou, dix-huit cent – eighteen

hundred. Work all dates that are hundreds; 1000, 1100, 1200, etc., and dates to 1000.

1801 mille huit cents un – (one) thousand eight hundred one, ou dix-huit cent un

1810. mille huit cents dix – (one) thousand eight hundred ten …etc.

1870. mille huit cents soixante-dix – (one) thousand eight hundred sixty plus ten

1871. mille huit cents soixante et onze – (one) thousand eight hundred plus eleven

1872 mille huit cents soixante-douze – (one) thousand eight hundred and twelve

...continue

1875. mille huit cents soixante quinze – (one) thousand eight hundred seventy-five. ou, dis-huit-soixante-quinze. 'dix-huit' =18, 'soixant-quinze' – sixty+fifteen = 75

...continue

1877. mille huit cent soixante-dix-sept – (one) thousand eight hundred seventy-seven 60+10+7 (77). Ou, quinze-trois soixante-dix-sept. 15+3=18 60+10+7=77

1880. mille huit cent quatre-vingts - one thousand eight hundred eighty 4(20)=80, ou, quinze-trois quatre-vingt. – eighteen eighty, ou, dix-huit quarte-vingt, 10+8 4(20)

1881. mille huit cent quatre-vingt et un – one thousand eight hundred eighty 4(20)+one

1882. mille huit cent quatre-vingt-deux – one thousand eight hundred eighty-two ou, quinze-trois quatre-vingt-deux

1890. mille huit cent quatre-vingt dix – one thousand eight hundred eighty + 10=90.

1891. mille huit cent quatre-vingt onze – one thousand eight hundred eleven

1897. mille huit cent quatre-vingt-dix-sept – thousand eight hundred - 100 800 4(20) + ten + seven = ninty-seven ou dix-huit quatre-vingts-dix-sept

...finish with the French vigesimal numbers.

1850. dix-huit cent cinqante [dizuwisasehkat] 18 100 50

1900. dix-neuf cent [diznewfsa]

1968. dix-neuf soixante huit [disnewfswasotewi]

Mai 1968 -The events of May 1968 came about when student protests, coupled with widespread industrial unrest, culminated in a general strike and rioting. De Galle's government survived the crisis, but the issues raised made the events a turning point in French social history. Ibid p 290).

1950. dix-neuf cent cinquant [dixnewfsasehkat], ou, dix-neuf cinquant

2000. deux mille [dewmil]

2021. deux mille vingt et un [dewmilvaheju] (j=y)

2022. deux mille vingt-deux - 2000 22. [dewmilvahdew] ou, vingt vingt-deux – 20 22. [vahvahdew]

Work with dates two ways: thousands, hundreds - then first pair + second pair.

Section VI: Birthdates (anniversaire)

January 22, 1856 – vingt-deux Janvier [zahvjr] dix-huit-cent cinquante-six [vahdew zavjerdizuisikat] vingt-deux – 20+2=22 Janvier dix-huit cent – 10+8=18+100 cinquante-six –ou, mille huit cent cinqante-six.

February 19, 1999 – dix-neuf février, [fevriewr] mille neuf cent quatre-vingt dix-neuf, ou, quinze-quatre quatre-vingt dix-neuf – 15+4 =19, 4(20) 80 + 10 + 9

March 25, 2021 – vingt-cinq [vah-sah] mars [mers] deux-mille vingt et un [marz dewmil vah e jun], ou, mars vingt vingt et un 20 21.

April 15, 1890 – quinze avril, mil dix-huit cent quatre-vingt dix – 1000-800-4(20)+10, ou, quinze-trois (15+3) 4(20)+10. [avril] The 'r' in French is pronounce with tongue on lower teeth. Ask a browser, 'how to pronounce the French 'r'.

May 31, 1990 – trent-un mai [meh], mil neuf cent quatre-vingt dix, ou, quinze-neuf quatre-vingt dix. – 15 + 9 4(20) + 10.

June 1, 1899 – un juin [zuah], mil huit cent (1000 800) quatre-vingt dix neuf – 4(20) + 10 + 9, ou, trente huit (8 +10) quatre-vingt dix neuf, 4(20) + (10+9) = 80 +19.

July 30, 1933 – trente juilliet [zulje], mil neuf cent trente-trois. ou, dix-neuf trente-trois. [trahtzuwilye, milnewfsatraht-trwa] – write the numbers. *Toujours* !

August 14, 1750 – dis-quatre août [u] , mil sept cent cinquante. Ou, dix-sept cinquante.

September 9, 1610 – le neuf septembre [septahmbr], mil six cent dix. [leneufseptahb, mil (1000) seize cent (600) dix (10)], ou, seize (16) dix (10).

October 18, 1790 – dix-hui octobre, [oktobr] mil sept cent, quatre-vingt-dix, 1700 + 80 + 10, ou, dix-sept quatre-vingt dix. (10 + 7 and 4(20) + 10

November 18, 1880 – dix-huit novembre [novahb] (10+8), ou quinze-trois (15+3), ou mille huit-cent dix-huit.

December 25, 2000 – vingt-cinq [vahsah] décembre deux-mille, ou, noël deux mille – Christmas 2000. [decahbdewmil]

The afore going numbers and dates are not so much memory as they are math logic. Once you understand the logic, numbers and dates then have only to be practiced. So, make up birthdates, and historical numbers and work them out. You will master them with work. ...you must !

Section VII: More with numbers

Question : How many ? – Combien? [kobja] (j is pronounced as 'y')

Réponse : One, please. – u [ew, œ] [yn] - before a vowel or mute 'h', s'il vous plais. – deux, s'il vous plais, etc.. work them on up. Be able to say the phrase 1-20, or more without the book, i.e. by memory. Include, 'combien', [kobja]

Combien un douzaine - dozen. [combja uduzay], ou demi-douzaine. Half dozen. Combien fait une demi-douzaine ? [combiefay ewdemidozain] – 'fait' comes from 'faire', to make, 3rd person 'it makes' – lit. How much it makes a half-dozen ?, ou, How much is a half-dozen ?

Combien pour deux? [combiepewrdew] – How much for two?

Combien pour deux douzaines? [combiepewrdewdozain] – how much for two dozen?

Talk these phrases with more (dozens) higher. *Improviser et parler* !

Question: Is this your first time coming to Paris? - Est-ce la première fois que vous venez à paris? [ese lapremje fwa kevuvenzaparee]

Résponse: No, it's my second time. Non, c'est ma deuxième fois. [non, sesma dewzjemfwa] - 3rd time, 4th time, etc... do them!

Compare 'fois' with 'heure'... both mean 'time'. The distinction must be known and understood. Look 'em up!

Ordinal numbers are à englais, first, second, third, etc. – Cardinal numbers are à englais, one, two, three, etc.

première fois – c'est la première fois [sesla premjefwa] – ce n'est pas la première fois – It's not the first time. [senespa lpremjefwa] – It's not the first time. 'n'est is a contraction, 'is not'- 'ne' like 'la or le' is shortened to 'n' and 'l' before words beginning with a vowel. In French the verb, 'est' has two negatives, one on each side of the verb – 'ce n'est pas' – it's not... [senespa]

Ce n'est pas bien. [senespabie] This is not good. C'est très bien. [sestraybie] This is very good, ou, c'est bon, ou, c'est bien.

deuxiéme fois – c'est la deuxieme fois [seladewzjiemfwa] – It's the second time.

troisiéme fois – c'est la troisieme fois [selatrosiemfwa] – It's the third time.

Now improvise by using different Ordinal numbers to twenty.

premièr fois, deuxiéme fois, troisiéme fois, etc. c'est ma quatreiéme fois, etc.

Section VIII: Time of day

This is another area that you will use frequently. You will have occasions to ask what time it is, and you will reply with the time. Ideally, you would work with a partner, but if you are doing this alone, you take the part of the person asking, and the person replying, as before – comme tujour. [komtuzur]

French time is taken from military time as used by the military, scientists, law enforcement, firefighting, and emergency medical services. It starts at midnight as 0000 - zero hours, with 1:00am as 0100 hours, 2am as 0200 hours, etc to 1200 hours for noon, then 1300 hours for 1pm, 1400 hours for 2pm, etc., to 2300 hours for 11pm, then midnight as 0000 hours, or midnight.

From midnight - minuit – 0h00 'h' for 'heures, and replaces the colon. – 00:00 , to 00h00.

Quarter hours may be indicated with quinze, trente, (demi) or quarante-cinq. (15-30-45)

A quarter past midnight - minui et quart, 0h15, ou, quinze minuit. (quart=quinze)

Half-past midnight is 'minui et trent ou demi [minwietrat], '0h30'.

Forty-five minutes past midnight – minui-quarante-cinq, ou - a quarter to one – 'un heures moins le quart' [junewrmwalekar]. '0h45'. – 'j'=y, [yun] before mute 'h' or a vowel.

Look up 'moins'...

1am – un heure du matin 1h [junewrdumata] – Look up 'matin' and its uses.

1:10 – un heure dix du matin 1h10 [junewrdisdumata]

1:15 – un heure quinze du matin 1h15 [junewrkezdumata]

1:30 – un heure trent du matin 1h30 [junewrtrentdumata]

1:45 – un heure quarante-cinq ou, deux moins le quart [junewr karatsankdumata]

2:00 - deux heures du matin 02h [dewewrdumata]

2:15– deux heures quinz du matin. 02h15 [dewewrkeysdumata] etc..

2:30 – deux heures trent du matin. 02h30 [dewewrtrantdumata]

2:45– deux heures quarante-cinq. 02h45 ou, trois heures moins le quart – quarter to three. [dewewrkarantsank] ou [trwaewrmwalekar]

03h00 – trois heures [trwaewr]

Continue through the morning hours with quarter hours. Telling time by the minute should be no problem. Practice full sentences; quell heure est-il ? Il est cinq heures du matin, ou, Il est cinq. Say the whole sentences with varying hours, and do it frequently. This is French! - Live French – vivre la française! [vivrlafransay]

From noon ...

Quarter hours may be indicated with quinze, trente, or quarante-cinq. (15-30-45)

A quarter past noon, 'midi et quart' ou, douz heures et quart après-midi 12h15,

Half past noon - midi et demie, ou, trent - 12h30

1pm - treize heures, 13h ou, 'un heures après midi' [jewnewr apraymidi]

1:15 treize heures quartre après-midi [trizewrkat] 13h15

1:30 un heure trent après-midi 13h30, ou, treize heures demi

1:45 treize heures quarante-cinq 13h45 ou, deux heures moins le quart – a quarter to two.

2:00 quatortze heures 14h00

...continuez [kotinu]

Question: [kesteo] What time is it? Quelle huere est-il? [kelewresil] Do some research on these words. Understand that 'h' is not pronounced. Looking up 'quelle' you find 'quel' is followed with 'quelle' as an (interrog), a question; what or who. As an excl, 'quelle' [kel] is 'Surprize!', ou, 'what a surprise!' Look it up… comme toujours!

Résponse: It's one minute past noon. - Il est midi une minute. [ilesmidiuminu] ou midi deux… etc., learn them all. Improvise! The word, 'passé' may be used three different ways; 1. As an *adj*; le mois passé [lemwa pasay] – last month. Il est huit heures passés [iles huit ewr pasay] – It is past eight o'clock. 2. As a *prep* after – passé six heures [pasay sisewr] – after six o'clock. And, passé cette maison [pasay cetmaiso] – past this house. And, quel est votre passé-temps? [keles votr pasay-tamp] – What is your past-time? This gives you many improv possibilities! - found in your dictionaries.

Question: What time do you have, mom? - Quelle huere as-tu, maman? [kelewr astumama] – ou, avez-vous l'heure, monsieur? [avevu l'ewr, msewr] Literally, what time have you, ou do you have the time? Add 'monsieur', 'madam', et 'mademoiselle', and names of French people. Parler française! In English we say 'whatimsit ?' …or something like that, but surely not, 'What time is it' – each word separately. As in any language, words get melded together and one is aware of the phrase as a unit, not so much each individual word or letter. So meld the above phrases together and we have, [kelewrastu], ou [avevulewr], quickly without effort. Check your pronunciation in 'reverso' or any other translators.

Résponse : 'Il est treize heure' [iles trayz ewr], ou 'Il est 13h'. 'It's 1pm' ou 'It's 1300 hours'. Then 2pm, 3pm, etc with ordinal numbers. They must be écrit et parlé [aykri eparlay]- written and spoken.

Question: Quelle heure as-tu? [kel ewr astu], ou, 'Quelle heure avez-vous ? Récherche la différance !

Résponse : J'ai (I have…) Morning or after-noon can be specified if necessary ; Il est un heure. [iles un ewr] ou, il est un heure du matin – It's 1am [ilesunewr dumatay] 1h00, written. Then '2h du matin', 3h du matin', etc… 'Il est deux heure du matin' [iles dew ewr dumatay] – '…trois heure [trwaewr] …quatre heure [katr ewr], etc.. Aussi bien que… Il est un (heures) apres-midi – It's 1pm, etc… Improvise with all clock numbers, write them down and make sentences from them based upon the examples above. Get them down cold! This is an important part of speaking French. parler, parler, parler! [parle], et parlez plus fort! [parleplufor] …et parle plu souvent ! Look 'em up… étudier!

Question: What time is it, ou what time do you have? – Quelle heure est-il, ou, as-tu, ou, avez-vous. Look 'em up, or with a translator..

Résponse: It's one o'clock in the afternoon. – Il est une heure de l'après midi. and, Il est six heure du soir.

[eelessisewrduswar]...etc to 'onze heure'. Note that 'apres midi' and 'du soir' are interchangeable depending on what you consider afternoon or evening. For example, 'six o'clock' maybe 'après midi', or 'du soir'.

Question: Is it one o'clock yet? – Es-il encore une heure?

[esilakorunewr]

Réponse: No, it's one-ten, sir. - Non, il est un heure dix, monsieur. [eelesewewerdis mesewer] ...add other names and proper names.

Improvise on the above with various times; 'two-fifteen', 'five-seven', etc.

Now for the 'am' – before noon numbers...

Question: Is it midnight? – est-ce minuit? [esce minui]

Résponse: 'It's midnight' – 'C'est minuit' [sesminui]. 'Is it midnight already? – Est-il déjà minuit? [esil dayshaminui?] Presque! [presk] Almost!

Question: Est-ce après minuit? – Is it after midnight ?

Réponse: Oui, il est minuit quinze. i.e. midnight + fifteen. ou…
Il est douze heures quinze. - i.e. two-fifteen. (for either am or
pm) ou 'Il est douze heures et quart'

Noon – midi 1pm – 13h or 'il est une heure' ou 'il est une
heure apres-midi' 1:30 pm – 'une heure trente'. ou 13h30. Take
it all around the clock to minuit. All time indications must
contain 'heure' (h), viz.. 13h30, not just 'one-thirty' – 1:30.
Time is usually indicated with the 24 hour clock. – 13h, 14h to
23h – 13h10 is 1:10pm, with minutes as needed. 13h00 is an
indication that it is 13h without any minutes. 23h is the last
because 24 is minui, midnight - 0000. After noon time can be
expresses as une heure aprés-midi to 6pm when aprés-midi
becomes soir (evening). 6pm the can be expressed either 'six
heures aprés-midi' or 'six heures du soir'. When it's headed for
evening 'soir' is sometimes used: '5 heures du soir' – cinq
heures du soir. Use either aprés-midi or soir, nuit (night) is
possible ; 'onze heure à nuit' - 11 at night. 'La nuit de Noël' is
Christmas eve. And, 'matinée' is afternoon cinema, or
performance, et danse-matinée.

Midnight – minuit 1am 'une heure du matin' ou '1h du matin'
1h15 du matin (1:15am) '1h30 du matin', (1:30am) 2h – deux
heures, 3h - trois heures, etc. Take it all the way to onze heures
with varying minutes. Starting at 2:00am – 02h00 '02' will
indicate morning. '00' is zero minutes. '02h10' is 2:10am.

Note: precede each time with 'Il est (It is) as in, 'Il est un
heure du matin'

Also, work the quarter hours – 13h15 et quart – 13h30 – 13h45
trois quarts. – Quarter past 1, 13h15, - Half past 13h30, Three
quarters past 13h45. Conversely, quarter to 1 – '1h45 douze
heures moins le quart'. 'Deux heures moins le quart'- quarter to
one. etc… quart – trent/demi – quarte/cinq, or moins le quart.- a
quarter to the next time. So, it's either 1:45, or its a quarter to
two. - Il est treize heures quarante-cinq, ou Il est quatorze
heures moins le quart.

à l'heure – on time - toujour `à l'heure – always on time

C'est l'heure – It's time, time's up! 'le heure' is contracted to
'l'heure as it is with words beginning with 'h'.

Section IX: Anniversaries

The anniversaire is the yearly anniversary, a birth date, founding, passing anniversary, etc. It is expressed in ordinal numbers. 'The company comes to celebrate it's fiftieth anniversary'. - 'L'entreprise vient le fêter son cinquantième anniversaire.' [l'atrepri venlefet so sekatjem aniverser] Search in your browser, 'vient le fêter', et étudier. 'I just passed my thirty-fifth birthday' – 'Je viens de passer mon trent-cinquième anniversaire' [zheven depasr mopase trat-sankjem aniverser] Browse 'viens' to find the root word (it won't be found in your dictionary) Make a note of it and its conjugation, found in Larousse French dictionary, central blue section, or reverso – just ask !

May 15, 1889 the Eifel Tower opened to the public, and was the main attraction of the Universal Exhibition In Paris. May 15, 2003 is its 134th anniversary. – le deux mille deux mai sera le cent trente-troisiéme anniversaire le tour Eiffel.

July 14, 1789 is the date the storming of the Bastille, a medieval fortress used as a state prison and became a symbol of the harsh rule of the Bourbon monarchy. It resulted in the end of the 'ancient régime'. July 14th of each year is the Bastille Day, a national holliday. 2023 will be its 234th anniversary. – le quatorze juillet, sera son deux cent trent-troisiéme anniversaire.

Section X: French math

There will be times where you might need to express yourself with basic arithmetic, or know what someone is doing when they express themselves in the same manner.

Again, there will be words that you have had, and words that you don't know. Look them all up and acquaint yourself with the basics. Comme toujours! [komtuzur]

Addition... First off, this gives a wonderful opportunity to work the numbers. There are two words that need to be learned: 'font' and 'égal'. 'font' is a verb and if you look it up you won't find it because it is not a 'root', or 'infinitive' verb, so ask your browser to 'conjugate font', and you will find it as 'faire', to make - in the column for 3rd person, 'they make'. Lit., two plus two, they make four. (ils font). So, 'deux plus un font trois' – two plus one make three etc. Take this on up and add many numbers. Get used to them. – 'quatre plus cinq font neuf', 'huit plus neuf font dix-sept' etc. It's fairly easy. There is an alternate way to express addition; 'un plus un égal deux'. 'égal' is 'equals', 'un plus cinq égal six', etc.

Now 'improviser' by adding many different numbers. 2 plus 3 = 5, - deux plus trois font cinq, ou deux plus trois égal cinq. Font 'make', and 'égal' equal. *Pas difficile* ! That's it for addition in French. Oh, Do some higher numbers...

Subtraction is just as easy. 'Two minus one is one' – deux moins un est un. 'moins' should be a familiar word since we had that word in 'a quarter to three', ou 2:45. – trois heures moins le quart. - moins is less', so 'moins le quart' is less by a quarter. In number subtraction 'moins' is also used; 'cinq moins quatre font un'. In addition to 'moins', you have 'font' – lit. they are, or just 'is', so 'cinq moins quatre font un' – five minus four is one. We could also say, 'cinq moins quatre égal un' – five minus four equals one. Talk about choices! Drill yourself and *improviser* to your heart's content! Spell 'moins' correctly, and don't confuse with 'mont' ou, 'mois' – *look 'em up* ! Ok, one more…

Division is just a little bit more… 'cinq divisé par deux fait deux et demi' – five divided by two is two and a half. 'fait' is the present tense of 'faire' the infinitive, 'it makes…', or 'is…', five divided by two makes two and a half, or …is two and a half. 'Neuf divisé par tois égal trois.' – nine divided by three is three. Work division to your heart's content! And finally…

Multiplication 'quatre fois quatre font sieze'. 'fois' is times and 'font' is 'is', or 'makes'. Then you can choose 'égal' instead of 'font', as before. Four times four makes (is) sixteen, ou, four times four is equal to sixteen. – 'quatre fois quatre égal sieze'.

Not only is this improvising French, but improvising numbers ad lib ! The more you do, the more you will be able to speak French ! There are no short-cuts. It simply takes a lot of work, but as you go, the French word, terms, or phrases will just be there. Won't that be nice ?

Section XI: French Restaurant

Calling…

Question: bonjour ? Est-ce [esse]…(restaruant)? – Is this…(restaurant)

Réponse : Oui, monsieure. Combien de personnes s'il vous plais? [combyedeperson s'eelvooplay] How many people, please?

Réponse : Deux, ma épouse et moi. [dew, aypuz emwa] Improvise with more/different people… (epouse, similar to 'spouse'. Ending with 'e' is feminine – 'epoux' is masc.

Question: Puies-je vous aider, monsieur? [pueezevooaide, mesewr] – May I help you, sir? 'aider', 'help' – m'aider – 'help me' is the term from which we get 'mayday, mayday, mayday' (always three) – extreme help, emergency!

Résponse : Oui, merci. [owee, mercee] Yes, thank you.

Question: Vin? [vah] Wine

Résponse: Oui. [owee] Yes

Question: Avez-vous un vin rouge léger ? [avayvoo uvah rouze layzer], 'Do you have a light red wine?'. Lit. 'Do you have a wine red light ?' Adjectives come after the noun in French. Rechearche 'rouge' including 'moulin rouge', and 'moulin è vent'.

Résponse : je suis désolé, non. [zhe swee, dayzolay, noh] 'I'm sorry, no.'

Question: un bon vin blanc léger? [uvah bo blah layzer] – A good light white wine?

Résponse: Oui, vin sec ou doux? [ewee, vah sec ou duw] – dry or sweet

Résponse: très sec, monsieur! [traysec msewer] – very dry …ou 'doux'… [o duz]… or sweet.

Résponse: très bien monsieur!! [traybieh msewer] – very good, sir.

Question : What is the better wine? – quell est le meilleur vin? [keles le meyewr vah] – white wine - vin blanc, red wine, - vin rouge. (The adjective comes after the noun)

Résponse: I would like a glass of red/white wine. – je voudrais une verra du vin rouge/blanc [zhe vodray u ver du vah rouze/blah] Look up the several uses of 'blanc', as well as other words. *étudier*! 'pronounces-le correctement s'il vous plaise ! Write out your pronunciation guide between brackets [   ] according to what you hear in a sound bite. étudier la prononciation ! – not just here, but everywhere ! – 'pas seuelement, mais partout'

Question: Où sont les entrées ? [oosah lay ahtray] Where are the main courses ?

Résponse: dans la troisième page, monsieur. [da lu twaziaim pashz, mesewr], ou 'première, ou, 'deuxième', ou 'quatrième, etc… Be sure to look up pronunciations for all ordinal numbers. Call off the page numbers in a magazine… all of them! And do it often. It's the only way you will learn and have them stick. – premier page, deuxiéme page, troisiéme page, and pronounce them – premje paz, dewsjem paz, trwasjem paz, etc…

Question: Avez-vous dessert, monsieur? [avayvoodezer,mesiewr- Do you have deserts, sir?

Résponse : Oui, il sont a la dernière page. [owee, eelsohaladernyerpazsh] – Yes, they are on the last/final page. In Paris there is a café called, 'La Durnière Goutte' – 'The Last Drop' [la durnyer goot] featuring wine tasting Saturdays. Search for it on your browser – there are pictures of the café. Ask your browser. …e rechearche de films français et youtube French for virtual walking tours through various French cities including La Basillique du Sacrè-CŒur de Montmartre, et la Champ Elysée. And, 'Snippets of Paris' is a totally delightful site…*Aller* !

Make a list of words and phrases that you know and can actually use, so that you can continue to use and expand, and improvise on them choosing names, words or adding phrases, viz, 'comment vas-tu, Marie? ...'ca va', ou 'pas très bien', ou 'très bien, merci', etc.. Adding a name makes all the difference in the world, as does, 'Bonjour Marie', ou, monseieur/juene homme/mademoiselle/mesdemoiselles, etc.. Anything in question, *recherche*! ...e entraînez-vous à la prononciation! [e ahtranevu a la pronahsiassha]. Look up entrée, esp as (culin). Note that similar words in French and English have different spellings and well as pronunciations, 'question' for one [kestjo], has the same spelling. Many French sound-bites are very fast, and you must listen carefully to get the pronunciation. French is spoken quickly.

Section XII: French Food Terms

The French chef is the 'cuisinier français' [quisinjer fransay]
Look up 'chef' for it's several uses. Then look up 'cuisine'.
Most words have more than one usage, therefore it's obviously
good to know these usages. One may ask, 'who is your chef? –
'Qui est ton chef'[kiestoshef], which really asks who is your
owner, or boss? – or, 'Qui est ton cuisinier?', [kies ton
quisinjer] which is asking who is your cook? You might also
ask, 'Who is your head cook?' – Qui est votre chef cuisinier?'
Get an idea of the meanings of the two words, and create
sentences using each by researching in your dictionary. For
example, 'My wife is boss' – Ma femme est chef'. 'He is head
of his unit' – Il est chef de son unité. [ilesshefdesonunitay]. 'She
is the conductor of the orchestra' – elle est chef d'orchestre.
[elesshefdorkestr]. Livre de cuisine. – cookbook, [livrdkwisin]
ou livre de recettes [livrdreset] – book of recepes (cookbook).

French food is an art, and the cuisinier is an artist. The owner of
a restaurant is its chef, and in many cases its cuisinier (cook).

French wines are reguated by the AOC - Appellation d'Origine
Contrôlée and refers to standards set for wines made in France.

French wines are of many varieties, types, and qualities. The
main French regions are: Alsace, Armagnac and Cognac,
Beaujolais and Lyonaise, Bordeaux, Burgundy, Champagne,

Corsica, Jura, Languedoc, Lorraine, Bourgogne, Chablis, Côte de Nuits, Côte Chalinnaise, Macounais, Beaujolais, and others.

WineFolly is a great site for an explanation of terms regarding French wines. Due to climate change, vineyards have moved north, or up where cooler temperatures are more conducive to fine wine grapes. French wine is having a difficult with it, but are surviving. Surprisingly, England is producing excellent wines that are served at all official gatherings. English beer is having a tough time of it, again because of climate change.

Section XIII: The euro: €

France is a founding member of the European Union (EU) and one of the first countries to adopt the euro on 1 January, 1999. The French franc was no longer in use by 17 February 2012. – dix-sept février vingt dix-deux.

Bank notes come in amounts of €5, €10, €20, €50, €100, €500

Coins come in amounts of 1c, 2c, 5c, 10c, 20c, 50c (centimes) and €1, and €2

Most places accept Visa or MasterCard, but ask. – acceptez vous les cartes de crédit ?

The comma vergule (,) is used in the place of the period (.) vis; €10,50 – ten euros and fifty centimes. In English the euro sign comes before the amount: €20,10. In France it comes after the amount: 20,10 €. Do not confuse 'cent' in French with USD 'cent'. *Recherche !*

Question: How much is the umbrella? – combien coûte le parapluie? [combja ku le parapli]

Response: Il en coûte dix euro, cinquante – It costs ten euros and fifty centimes–10,50 € 'dix euros cinqante' [dis euros saykat]

Euros and centimes are calculated much like dollars and cents in English. Thus, 10,99 € would be written in USD, $10.99. The French comma, ',' is a vergule that replaces the English period '.' in numbers relating to costs. 'ça coute dix euros quatre-vingt dix neuf'. 'combien' [combya] 'how much', and 'ça coûte' [sa cu] 'it costs' are the basic terms when shopping, along with amounts in euros.

Euros should be no problem since euros and centimes are calculated the same as dollars and cents. The math is the same.

Section XIV: Conclusion

You have come to the end of Book I Speak French Now.
Congratulations! Actually, you have not come to an end, but to
a beginning. Your work in learning the French language has
only begun !

Review each part and put your improv abilities to work by
using sentences to expand upon, change, reduce... whatever...
but make sure you are not just 'memorizing' by taking each
phrase without improvising upon it. Learning *requires*
improvisation, not just memorizing. Use the sentences
frequently and they will be automatically memorized. And,
looking up a new French word, be sure to use it in two or three
different sentences, just as you would do with unfamiliar
English words. Use a translator to help create sentences. Then
be sure you understand every word in the translation. If not,
take some time to do some research on the words. Dictionary
definitions will have sentences within the definition that help
define the word. Words have not only different definitions, but
different usages as well. A word may change its part of speech
with its different definition.

Speak French Now, Book II will enlarge your French by taking
up the French verb, especially present, past, future, and
conditional tenses. In addition, the French pronoun is a subject

in-and-of itself, and is included with many possibilities for improvisation.

Talk French Now Book III covers a very powerful learning tool; the translation of French literature by writers Flaubert, Sagan, Voltaire and Dumas. You will learn how to learn French by translating French !

FIN

Printed in Great Britain
by Amazon

37316352R00036